MAD LIBS

CHRISTMAS CARDS

by P. Sean O'Kane

MAD LIBS
An Imprint of Penguin Random House LLC, New York

Mad Libs format and text copyright © 2020 by Penguin Random House LLC. All rights reserved.

Concept created by Roger Price & Leonard Stern

Cover illustration by Scott Brooks

Image credits: back cover: (snowflake pattern) ksugas/iStock/Getty Images;
stationery patterns: (snowman pattern) misspin/iStock/Getty Images, (penguins pattern) MirgoGrafiks/iStock/Getty Images,
(Christmas decorations pattern) Para-Graph/iStock/Getty Images, (Christmas town pattern) Tharnthip/iStock/Getty Images

Published by Mad Libs,
an imprint of Penguin Random House LLC, New York.
Manufactured in China.

Visit us online at www.penguinrandomhouse.com.

ISBN 9780593222096
3 5 7 9 10 8 6 4 2

MAD●LIBS®

INSTRUCTIONS

Everyone loves receiving cheerful and hilarious greetings during the holidays. But if you're not sure how to make the season merry and bright, don't worry. Mad Libs is here to help with this collection of 21 Mad Libs holiday cards that you can send to your friends and family! And the best part is, each one is guaranteed to knock their stockings right off the chimney. Here's how to make your own totally original holiday cards:

Step 1: Fill in the blanks. You can do this by filling in the missing words whenever you see a blank OR you can complete the blanks with help from a friend or nearby elf. First, choose a card from inside this book and ask your elf (or friend) to call out: "Give me a noun," "Give me an adjective," or whatever type of word the blank space asks for. Have the elf write down your answers in the blank spaces. Then, you're ready for step 2! There's an example of a partially complete Mad Libs on the back cover of this book, if you need it.

Step 2: Tear out the card carefully, fold it in half (see diagram below), seal it with a Mad Libs sticker, write in the name and address of the person receiving the card, put a stamp in the box provided, and drop the card in your local mailbox or a passing sleigh! Then, sit back and wait for the holiday cheer to begin!

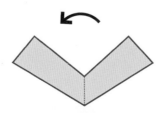

In case you have forgotten what adjectives, adverbs, nouns, and verbs are, here is a quick review:

An ADJECTIVE describes something or somebody. *Lumpy, soft, ugly, messy,* and *short* are adjectives.

An ADVERB tells how something is done. It modifies a verb and usually ends in "ly." *Modestly, stupidly, greedily,* and *carefully* are adverbs.

A NOUN is the name of a person, place, or thing. *Sidewalk, umbrella, bridle, bathtub,* and *nose* are nouns.

A VERB is an action word. *Run, pitch, jump,* and *swim* are verbs. Put the verbs in past tense if the directions say PAST TENSE. *Ran, pitched, jumped,* and *swam* are verbs in the past tense.

When we ask for A PLACE, we mean any sort of place: a country or city (*Spain, Cleveland*) or a room (*bathroom, kitchen*).

An EXCLAMATION or SILLY WORD is any sort of funny sound, gasp, grunt, or outcry, like *Wow!, Ouch!, Whomp!, Ick!,* and *Gadzooks!*

When we ask for specific words, like a NUMBER, a COLOR, an ANIMAL, or a PART OF THE BODY, we mean a word that is one of those things, like *seven, blue, horse,* or *head*.

When we ask for a PLURAL, it means more than one. For example, *cat* pluralized is *cats*.

Dear _____,
NAME OF PERSON

Christmas is _____,
VERB ENDING IN "ING"

so _____ up the tree
VERB

and hang _____
ARTICLE OF CLOTHING (PLURAL)

on the _____ chimney.
ADJECTIVE

String twinkling _____
PLURAL NOUN

all along the holly wreath.

Wrap the _____ that you bought
PLURAL NOUN

and _____ them underneath.
VERB

Put out hot _____ and cookies,
TYPE OF LIQUID

so Santa _____ has a treat,
LAST NAME

and cut some _____ carrots
ADJECTIVE

for his _____ to eat.
ANIMAL (PLURAL)

With the _____ all ready,
TYPE OF BUILDING

then it's time to _____ off to bed
VERB

to dream of _____
CELEBRITY

all dressed in _____ and red.
COLOR

_____ wishes,
ADJECTIVE

_____
PERSON IN ROOM

MAD LIBS®   From CHRISTMAS CARDS MAD LIBS® • Copyright © 2020
by Penguin Random House LLC.

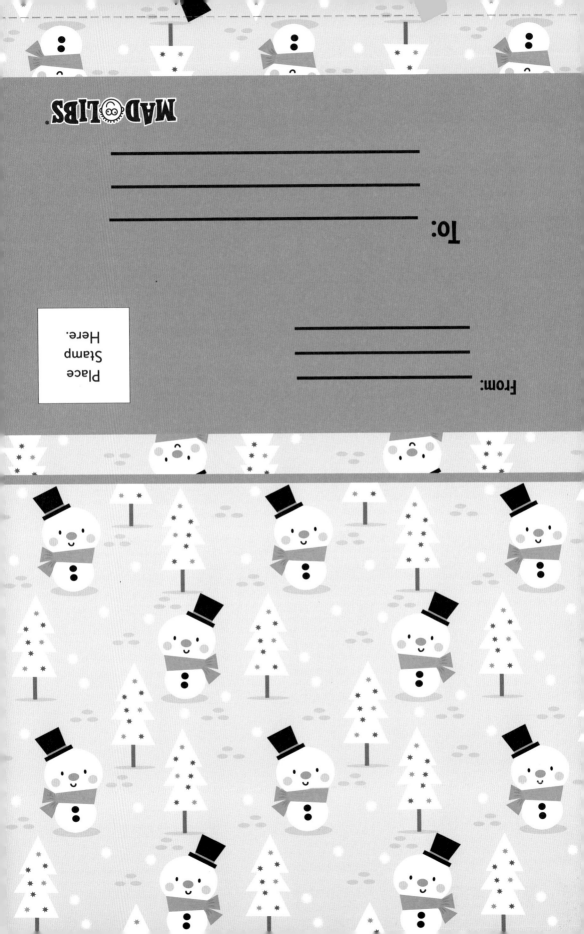

MAD LIBS

To:
_____
_____
_____

From:
_____
_____

Place Stamp Here.

Dear _____,
NAME OF PERSON

On the first day of Yuletide, I got a/an _____ so fair.
NOUN

On the second day, I got _____ for my hair.
PLURAL NOUN

On the third day, I got three bouncy _____,
PLURAL NOUN

on the fourth, a/an _____ teddy bear.
ADJECTIVE

On the fifth day, I got _____ _____ goats,
NUMBER   VERB ENDING IN "ING"

on the sixth, a/an _____ that floats.
NOUN

The seventh day brought me _____ _____,
ADJECTIVE   PLURAL NOUN

and the eighth, a/an _____ of oats.
TYPE OF CONTAINER

On day nine, I got a/an _____ ring.
COLOR

Day ten brought me _____ that sing!
OCCUPATION (PLURAL)

But day eleven will give me time with you,

which is by far my _____ thing!
ADJECTIVE

Merry _____,
TYPE OF EVENT

_____
PERSON IN ROOM

MAD LIBS®

To:

_____

_____

_____

From:

_____

_____

Place Stamp Here.

Dear _____,
NAME OF PERSON

I know this card isn't much,

just some _____ and some glue
NOUN

with a few _____ words inside
ADJECTIVE

and a festive _____ or two.
NOUN

But this card _____ for something bigger
VERB ENDING IN "S"

than any _____ envelope can hold.
ADJECTIVE

Something that money can't _____,
VERB

that's more precious than _____ or gold.
NOUN

It's a symbol of _____ wishes,
ADJECTIVE

_____ tidings, and holiday cheer.
ADJECTIVE

It's a/an _____ that says,
NOUN

" _____ Christmas to you
ADJECTIVE

and happy new _____!"
NOUN

_____ yours,
ADVERB

_____
PERSON IN ROOM

From CHRISTMAS CARDS MAD LIBS® • Copyright © 2020
by Penguin Random House LLC.

MAD@LIBS

To: _____
_____
_____

From: _____
_____

Place Stamp Here.

Dear _____,

NAME OF PERSON

Here are my top _____ things to do in the snow:

NUMBER

5. _____-ball fights!

NOUN

4. Going _____ down a hill!

VERB ENDING IN "ING"

3. Making snow _____!

OCCUPATION (PLURAL)

2. Catching snow-_____ on my _____.

PLURAL NOUN — PART OF THE BODY

1. Wishing you and your _____ a/an _____

NOUN — COLOR

Christmas this year!

_____ Christmas!

ADJECTIVE

_____,

ADVERB

_____

PERSON IN ROOM

MAD☺LIBS®

To:
_____
_____
_____

From:
_____
_____
_____

Place Stamp Here.

Dear _____,
NAME OF PERSON

It's Christmas all over the _____
NOUN

for as far as the _____ can see.
PART OF THE BODY

But nothing _____ better than being home
VERB ENDING IN "S"

to _____ _____ under the tree.
VERB   PLURAL NOUN

So light a/an _____ in the window
NOUN

to guide my _____-drawn sleigh.
ANIMAL

I'll be _____ Christmas carols
VERB ENDING IN "ING"

when I _____ on Christmas Day.
VERB

I'll shake my jingle _____
PLURAL NOUN

as my _____ _____ across the snow,
VEHICLE   VERB ENDING IN "S"

and yell to the horses, "_____,"
SILLY WORD

when there's no more distance to go.

_____ you soon,
VERB

_____
PERSON IN ROOM

MAD LIBS®   From CHRISTMAS CARDS MAD LIBS® • Copyright © 2020
by Penguin Random House LLC.

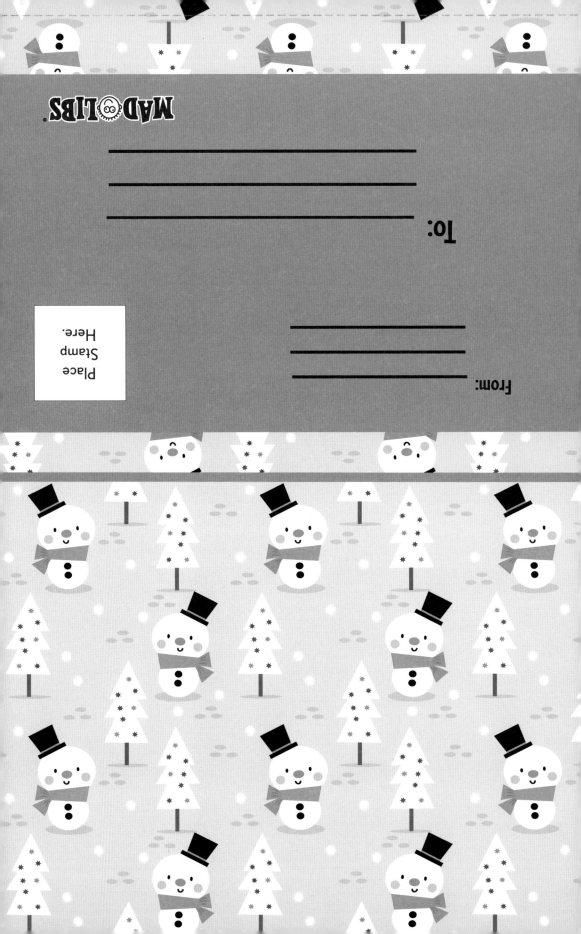

MAD LIBS

To: _____
_____
_____

From: _____
_____

Place Stamp Here.

Dear _____,
NAME OF PERSON

Happy _____! I'm _____ this note
PLURAL NOUN   VERB ENDING IN "ING"

because I _____ need your _____.
ADVERB   NOUN

Since Santa is always making _____ for everyone
PLURAL NOUN

else, I thought we could _____ him a present from us
VERB

this Christmas. Here are some ideas. I think Santa would like a

new flying _____ with _____ attached to
VEHICLE   PLURAL NOUN

the handlebars, a baby _____ named _____,
ANIMAL   SILLY WORD

or a vacation to (the) _____ for himself and
A PLACE

Mrs. _____. I hope you can _____,
LAST NAME   VERB

because Santa's been a very good _____ this
SOMETHING ALIVE

year!

Yours _____,
ADVERB

_____
PERSON IN ROOM

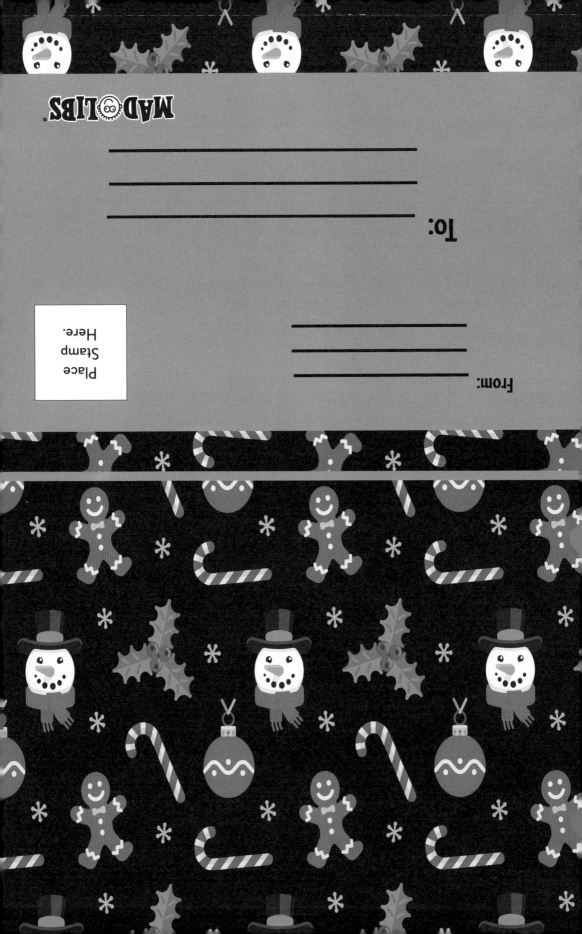

MAD☉LIBS®

To: _____
_____
_____

From: _____
_____

Place
Stamp
Here.

Dear _____,
NAME OF PERSON

Through the clouds Santa _____ on his sleigh,
VERB ENDING IN "S"

with his _____ _____ leading the way.
ADJECTIVE   ANIMAL (PLURAL)

Dasher is as fast as a/an _____ eagle in flight,
ADJECTIVE

while _____-er likes to party all night.
VERB

Prancer can do super-_____ kicks,
ADJECTIVE

and Vixen likes to _____ magic tricks.
VERB

Like a shooting _____, Comet flies in the sky,
NOUN

while Cupid winks at _____ nearby.
FIRST NAME

Donner can whinny "_____" very loud,
SILLY WORD

and Blitzen stands _____ and proud.
ADJECTIVE

Rudolph has a/an _____ _____ that glows,
COLOR   PART OF THE BODY

but that is a/an _____ everyone knows.
NOUN

There is one thing they all _____ to do,
VERB

and that's wish Merry Christmas to you!

Joy and _____ to you,
NOUN

_____
PERSON IN ROOM

MAD LIBS

To:
_____
_____
_____

From:
_____
_____

Place
Stamp
Here.

Dear _____,
　　　　　NAME OF PERSON

Wishing you a/an _____ new year
　　　　　　　　　　ADJECTIVE

full of _____ and fun.
　　　　　TYPE OF FOOD

May it bring you lots of _____,
　　　　　　　　　　　　PLURAL NOUN

and _____ by the ton.
　　　PLURAL NOUN

May your _____ friends give you _____
　　　　　ADJECTIVE　　　　　　　　　　　　NOUN

that you _____ in your heart.
　　　　　　VERB

And though life's road is _____,
　　　　　　　　　　　　ADJECTIVE

may our _____ never part.
　　　　　PLURAL NOUN

With memories in your _____
　　　　　　　　　　PART OF THE BODY (PLURAL)

of the _____ year that's passed,
　　　　ADJECTIVE

this year will be so _____,
　　　　　　　　　　ADJECTIVE

more _____ than the last.
　　　ADJECTIVE

In conclusion, let me _____
　　　　　　　　　　　VERB

and say it with zest:

May this new year bring you _____,
　　　　　　　　　　　　　NOUN

and all the very best.

All the _____,
　　　　　NOUN

_____
　　　PERSON IN ROOM

From CHRISTMAS CARDS MAD LIBS® • Copyright © 2020
by Penguin Random House LLC.

MAD LIBS®

To: _____
_____
_____

From: _____
_____

Place Stamp Here.

Dear _____,
NAME OF PERSON

I'm _____ the Snowman,
FIRST NAME

here to say to you,

I hope the season's full of _____
NOUN

and lots of _____ _____, too!
ADJECTIVE   PLURAL NOUN

From the top of my _____,
ARTICLE OF CLOTHING

to the bottom of my _____ snowball
ADJECTIVE

I came to _____ a happy holiday
VERB

to everyone, _____ and small!
ADJECTIVE

My _____ may be a carrot,
PART OF THE BODY

and my _____ may be coal,
PART OF THE BODY (PLURAL)

but inside I'm filled with _____
NOUN

and snow from the North Pole!

And though these _____ feelings
ADJECTIVE

are the only warmth I've felt,

it's _____ you a Merry Christmas
VERB ENDING IN "ING"

that makes my _____ melt!
PART OF THE BODY

Snowflakes and _____,
PLURAL NOUN

_____
PERSON IN ROOM

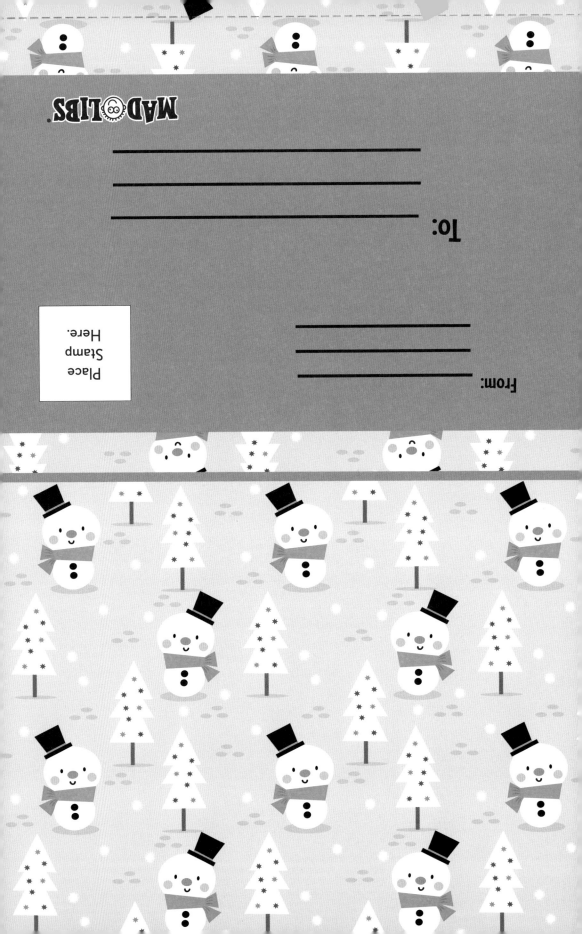

MAD LIBS

To:

_____

_____

_____

From:

_____

_____

_____

Place Stamp Here.

Aloha, _____,

NAME OF PERSON

The temperature is _____,

VERB ENDING IN "ING"

so let's both take a flight.

We'll celebrate Christmas in (the) _____,

A PLACE

where the _____ is clear and bright.

NOUN

While others freeze their _____ off

PART OF THE BODY (PLURAL)

and _____ in the heavy snow,

VERB

we'll be _____ in the sun

VERB ENDING IN "ING"

when to the beach we go.

We'll miss building a/an _____-man

NOUN

and _____ rides down the slope.

VEHICLE

But we'll see Santa _____ in swim trunks

VERB ENDING IN "ING"

while _____-skiing with a rope.

TYPE OF LIQUID

We'll snorkel with _____

ANIMAL (PLURAL)

and _____ to the coral reef,

VERB

and plan to _____ here next year

VERB

for some more winter relief!

Mele Kalikimaka,

_____

PERSON IN ROOM

From CHRISTMAS CARDS MAD LIBS® • Copyright © 2020 by Penguin Random House LLC.

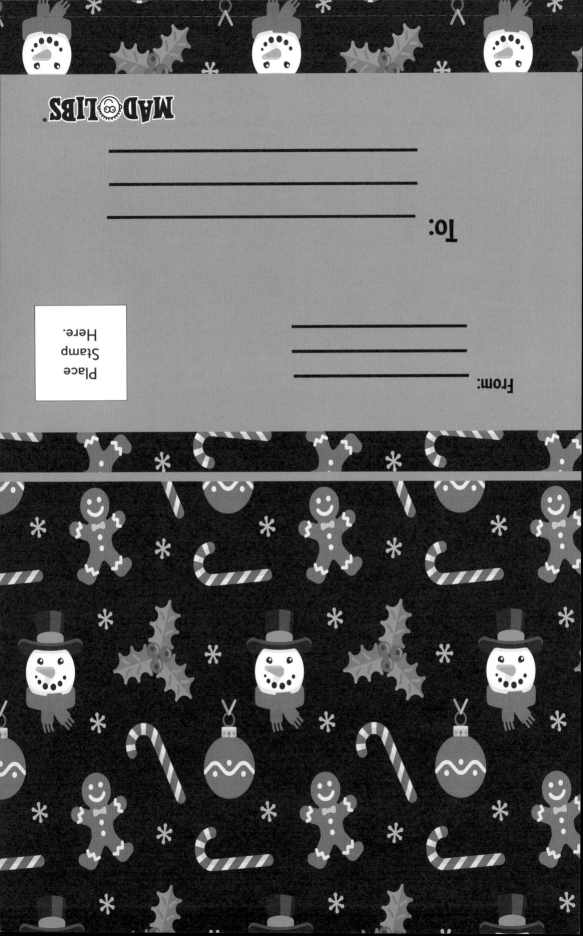

MAD◎LIBS®

To: _____
_____
_____

From: _____
_____

Place
Stamp
Here.

Dear _____,
NAME OF PERSON

What a year we've had at the _____ household!
LAST NAME

_____ graduated from (the) _____ and finally
FIRST NAME   A PLACE

got his _____'s license. Grandma spends most
OCCUPATION

of her time _____ in the _____ room.
VERB ENDING IN "ING"   ADJECTIVE

We took a vacation to (the) _____ and all came back
A PLACE

with sunburns on our _____. _____!
PART OF THE BODY (PLURAL)   EXCLAMATION

Then, _____ lost his wedding _____. Luckily,
FIRST NAME   NOUN

we were able to get it back from our pet _____,
ANIMAL

who had hidden it in his _____. Anyway, hope you are
NOUN

_____ the holiday season and are surrounded
VERB ENDING IN "ING"

by many good _____.
PLURAL NOUN

_____ holidays from the _____ family!
ADJECTIVE   SAME LAST NAME

MAD LIBS

To:

_____

_____

_____

From:

_____

_____

Place
Stamp
Here.

Dear _____,
NAME OF PERSON

Here, we decorate a Christmas _____,
NOUN

and in sunny _____, they have barbecues.
COUNTRY

Up in snowy _____, they get a Gävle _____;
COUNTRY   ANIMAL

in Iceland, yummy _____ in their shoes.
PLURAL NOUN

We sing _____ on Christmas Eve,
PLURAL NOUN

and in Japan they eat _____ chicken.
ADJECTIVE

But in Norway, they hide their _____
PLURAL NOUN

and no one sweeps the kitchen.

In El Salvador, they _____ fireworks
VERB

to have a/an _____ Christmas Day.
ADJECTIVE

In the dense _____ of Kenya, they speak Swahili.
PLURAL NOUN

"Heri ya Krismasi" is what they say.

The point is, my dear _____,
OCCUPATION

it doesn't matter where you live.

Christmas is the same all over,

a time to _____ and give.
VERB

With all the _____ in my _____,
NOUN   PART OF THE BODY

_____
PERSON IN ROOM

MAD☺LIBS®

To: _____
_____
_____

From: _____
_____

Place Stamp Here.

Dear _____,
NAME OF PERSON

In this season of saying thanks,

giving gifts, and _____ cheer,
ADJECTIVE

I think of all the wonderful _____
PLURAL NOUN

you give throughout the year.

Your talent for giving _____ is amazing.
PLURAL NOUN

You've made _____ good deeds an art.
VERB ENDING IN "ING"

Your kindness always _____
VERB ENDING IN "S"

my _____, _____ heart.
ADJECTIVE   SAME ADJECTIVE

You make every day shine like a/an _____.
NOUN

I'm so _____ because you're around.
ADJECTIVE

I'd give you a/an _____ medal if I could,
COLOR

and let the brass _____ sound.
PLURAL NOUN

You deserve _____ parades,
NUMBER

and your own tropical _____, too,
NOUN

because no Christmas _____ will ever be enough
NOUN

to say thanks for all you do!

Many _____,
PLURAL NOUN

_____
PERSON IN ROOM

From CHRISTMAS CARDS MAD LIBS® • Copyright © 2020
by Penguin Random House LLC.

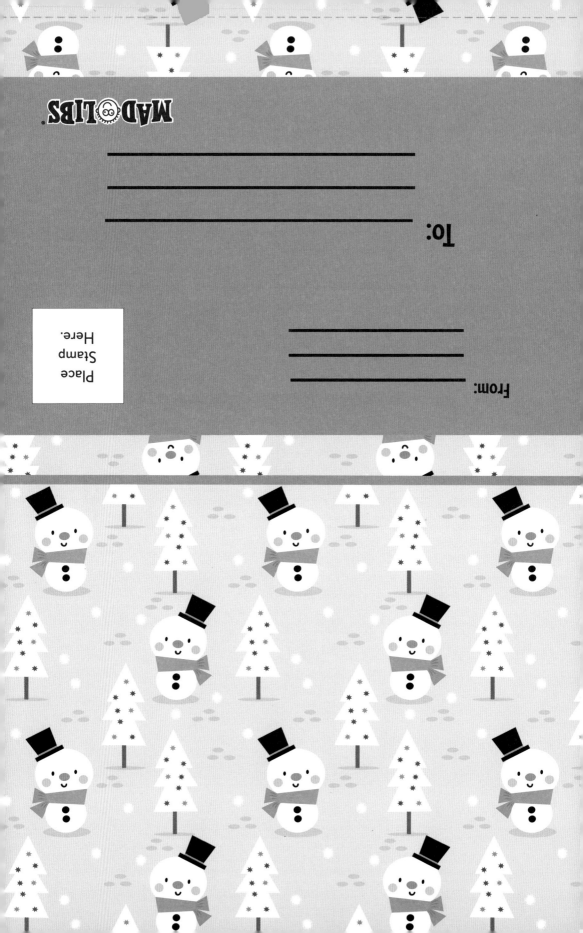

MAD○LIBS®

To: _____
_____
_____

From: _____
_____
_____

Place Stamp Here.

Dear _____,
NAME OF PERSON

Jingle bells are _____
VERB ENDING IN "ING"

from the _____ in the square!
TYPE OF BUILDING

Jingle _____ are ringing
PLURAL NOUN

from Santa's _____ flying in the air!
VEHICLE

_____ bells are ringing
ADJECTIVE

from my _____ as I climb the stairs!
ARTICLE OF CLOTHING

Jingle _____ are ringing
PLURAL NOUN

here, there, and everywhere!

I just wish they'd stop _____
VERB ENDING IN "ING"

for a minute or _____,
NUMBER

so I could wish a Merry Christmas to you!

Have a peaceful _____,
TYPE OF EVENT

_____
PERSON IN ROOM

MAD LIBS

To: _____
_____
_____

From: _____
_____

Place Stamp Here.

Dear _____,
NAME OF PERSON

As I decorate our Christmas _____
SOMETHING ALIVE

like a/an _____ elf,
ADJECTIVE

I think how this evergreen _____
NOUN

is like a gift itself.

The trunk is _____ and strong.
ADJECTIVE

We _____ it with such care.
VERB (PAST TENSE)

The needles smell so _____,
ADJECTIVE

_____ the smell of pine into the air.
VERB ENDING IN "ING"

The ornaments are hung _____,
ADVERB

so the branches don't bend,

by each beloved _____,
OCCUPATION

family member, and friend.

The garland _____ around the tree
VERB ENDING IN "S"

like the warmth we _____ each day.
VERB

The star on top shines _____
ADVERB

like a/an _____ to point the way.
NOUN

May your holiday season be _____,
ADJECTIVE

_____
PERSON IN ROOM

MAD○LIBS®

To: _____
_____
_____

From: _____
_____
_____

Place Stamp Here.

Dear _____,
NAME OF PERSON

A good _____ to you,
NOUN

and a happy _____ year!
ADJECTIVE

Let's celebrate like _____ stars
NOUN

with lots of _____ cheer.
ADJECTIVE

Next year, we'll pull out all the _____,
PLURAL NOUN

and _____ our old habits aside.
VERB

Start again fresh as a/an _____,
SOMETHING ALIVE

and take our _____ for a ride.
VEHICLE

We'll stop and _____ the roses,
VERB

and take a/an _____ in the sun.
NOUN

We'll aim _____,
ADVERB

take a/an _____, and then have some fun.
NOUN

We'll _____ a few eggs,
VERB

get _____ in the shade,
VERB (PAST TENSE)

and turn _____
TYPE OF FOOD (PLURAL)

into lemonade!

Merry Christmas and Happy _____!
PLURAL NOUN

_____
PERSON IN ROOM

From CHRISTMAS CARDS MAD LIBS® • Copyright © 2020 by Penguin Random House LLC.

MAD LIBS

To: _____

_____

_____

From: _____

_____

Place Stamp Here.

Dear _____,

"Ho! Ho! _____," says Santa Claus

on each _____ Christmas Day

to children who open their _____,

hoping he will stay.

They run down the _____

and _____ to the chimney,

finding Santa _____ gone,

and only _____ crumbs for them to see.

But if you listen _____

as he _____ by in his sleigh,

you'll hear him call out, "_____ and Merry Christmas,

be kind to all each day!"

And so I'm passing Santa's _____ of wisdom to you,

in case you're _____ in your bed

with dreams of sugar-_____

_____ in your head.

_____ Christmas!

_____

MAD LIBS

From CHRISTMAS CARDS MAD LIBS® • Copyright © 2020
by Penguin Random House LLC.

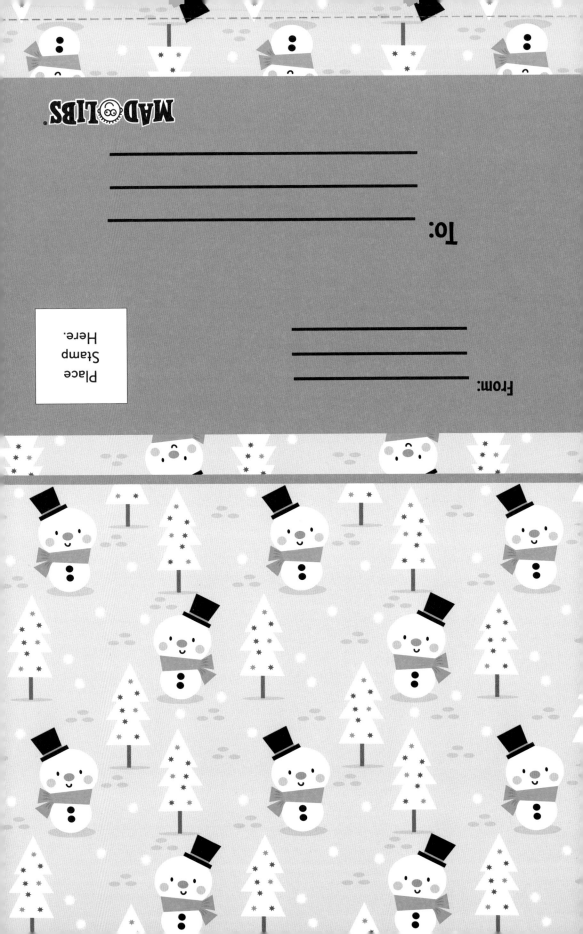

MAD LIBS®

To:
_____
_____
_____

From:
_____
_____
_____

Place
Stamp
Here.

Dear _____,
NAME OF PERSON

This is a Christmas wish

for every _____ _____ and boy.
ADJECTIVE   NOUN

May this _____ bring you happiness,
NOUN

lots of _____, and joy.
PLURAL NOUN

May it warm your _____,
PART OF THE BODY

and all that you hold dear.

May it _____ away your troubles
VERB

for the entire _____ year.
ADJECTIVE

So remember the good feelings you _____
VERB

on this Christmas night.

Let them always be with you,

and be your _____ light.
VERB ENDING IN "ING"

_____,
ADVERB

_____
PERSON IN ROOM

MAD☺LIBS®

To: _____
_____
_____

From: _____
_____

Place
Stamp
Here.

Dear _____,
NAME OF PERSON

Behind every Christmas present

is a/an _____ elf
ADJECTIVE

working in Santa's _____
TYPE OF BUILDING

or _____ on the shelf.
VERB ENDING IN "ING"

They sculpt and _____ and carve
VERB

all the _____ day through,
ADJECTIVE

making _____ toys
NUMBER

just for me and you.

Making _____ and wooden trains
PLURAL NOUN

and dolls is their _____ delight.
ADJECTIVE

They work as hard as _____
ANIMAL (PLURAL)

to be ready for Christmas night.

But what do these _____-working elves _____
ADVERB   VERB

when the work is all done?

They _____ back and watch
VERB

all the children _____ fun!
VERB ENDING IN "ING"

Hope you have a/an _____-filled Christmas,
NOUN

_____
PERSON IN ROOM

From CHRISTMAS CARDS MAD LIBS® • Copyright © 2020
by Penguin Random House LLC.

From: _____

_____

_____

Place
Stamp
Here.

To: _____

_____

_____

MAD LIBS

Dear _____,
NAME OF PERSON

'Twas the _____ after Christmas,
NOUN

and all through the _____,
TYPE OF BUILDING

all the creatures were _____,
VERB ENDING IN "ING"

even the _____.
ANIMAL

The _____ were hung by
ARTICLE OF CLOTHING (PLURAL)

the chimney without care,

in hopes that the _____ soon would be there.
OCCUPATION

Then from (the) _____, _____ heard
A PLACE PERSON IN ROOM

such a clatter,

I _____ from my bed and said, "What's the matter?"
VERB (PAST TENSE)

We went to the window and _____ it too hard,
VERB (PAST TENSE)

and saw a/an _____ sleigh still parked in our yard.
ADJECTIVE

"My reindeer broke down!" _____ Claus shouted
FIRST NAME

before he threw his _____ in the snow and pouted.
ARTICLE OF CLOTHING

Hope this Christmas is even better than last year!

_____,
NOUN

_____
PERSON IN ROOM

MAD☺LIBS®

To: _____
_____
_____

From: _____
_____

Dear _____!
NAME OF PERSON

_____ your favorite Christmas _____
VERB   NOUN
on the stereo!

Spin that disco _____,
NOUN
it's time to _____ up and go!
VERB

Santa's shaking his _____
PART OF THE BODY
all over the dance floor!

The elves are _____, too,
VERB ENDING IN "ING"
like they've never danced before!

D-_____ Rudolph
LETTER OF THE ALPHABET
is spinning a/an _____ beat!
ADJECTIVE
The rest of the _____ are lined up
ANIMAL (PLURAL)
in a conga line down the street!

We've got candy cane _____
TYPE OF LIQUID
and popcorn with _____ on top.
TYPE OF FOOD
Everyone's invited to come down and _____
VERB
'cause this party just won't stop!

Merry Christmas,

_____
PERSON IN ROOM

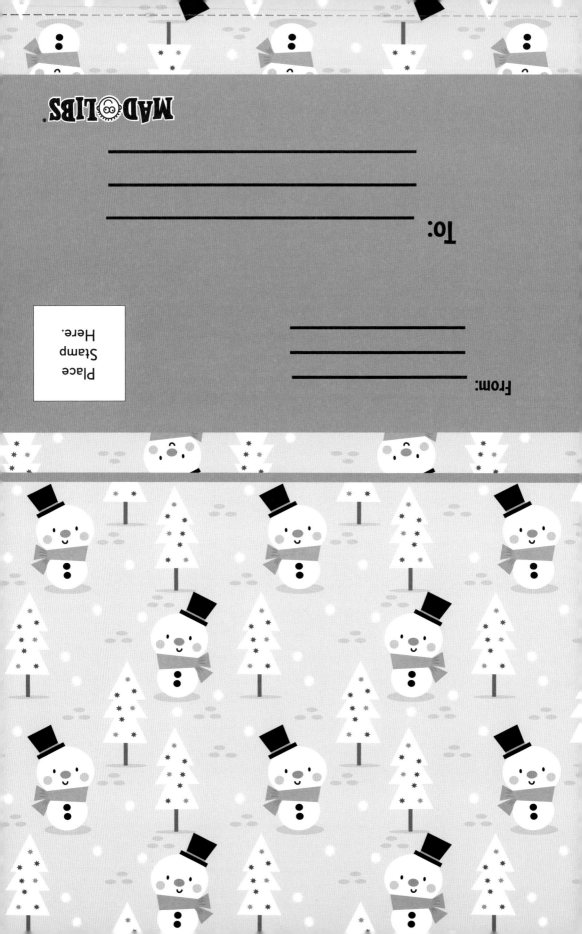

MAD☺LIBS®

To: _____

_____

_____

From: _____

_____

_____

Place Stamp Here.

Join the millions of Mad Libs fans creating wacky and wonderful stories on our apps!

Download Mad Libs today!